JOKES
TO TELL YOUR
WORST ENEMY

Books by Scott Corbett

The Deadly Hoax
Jokes To Read in the Dark
The Donkey Planet
The Discontented Ghost
The Lemonade Trick
The Disappearing Dog Trick
The Home Run Trick
The Hangman's Ghost Trick
Tree House Island
The Red Room Riddle
Here Lies the Body
Captain Butcher's Body
The Case of the Fugitive Firebug
The Case of the Ticklish Tooth
The Foolish Dinosaur Fiasco
What Makes a Car Go?
The Great McGoniggle's Key Play
Ever Ride a Dinosaur?
Bridges

SCOTT CORBETT

JOKES TO TELL YOUR WORST ENEMY

pictures by Annie Gusman

Published by The Trumpet Club
a division of Bantam Doubleday Dell Publishing Group, Inc.
666 Fifth Avenue, New York, New York 10103

ISBN: 0-440-84189-5

Reprinted by arrangement with E. P. Dutton,
a division of Penguin Books USA Inc.
Printed in the United States of America
February 1990

10 9 8 7 6 5 4 3
CW

for Barbara Summer
from Stanley Winters and me

INTRODUCTION

We all have worst enemies. I have six of them, all worst. You might say that is impossible, and you would be right, so don't say it.

Very well, now, do you want to make your worst enemy's life absolutely miserable? Do you want to do something horrible to him—or her? Good! That's the spirit! Well, first, sit him in a chair and tie him up good. Use plenty of rope, which may be purchased at any hardware store or ship chandler's. Tell them I sent you.

Now, here comes the worst part, guaranteed to make your worst enemy suffer tortures. It's simple.

Tell him these jokes! Or her.

Don't spare him or her a single one. Don't forget the really terrible Bad Joke on page 62, or maybe it's page 63—you'll know it when you come to it. And if you finally use up all these jokes, go back to my first book of terrible jokes, *Jokes To Read in the Dark*, in which I told you how to write bad jokes.

Don't you remember? Weren't you paying attention? How many times do I have to tell you these things?

Go to bed without any supper! And take this book with you.

WILLIAM
HALL

Here lies the body of William Hall
Who was 5 feet 11½ inches tall.
But now Bill and life have come asunder—
He was under 6 feet; now he's 6 feet under.

Q. Why did the elephant eat 100-watt bulbs?
A. It wanted a light lunch.

Q. What is the world's greatest milk shake?
A. A cow on a trampoline.

———•———

There once was a monster named Newsom
With a mean little brother named Hewsom;
    And once Hewsom grew some
    He made it a twosome—
And was even more gruesome than Newsom!

———•———

"I'm in the mood for True or False," said Stanley Winters. "Answer this. George Washington had his own teeth— True or False?"

"False!"

"I know they were false, but he still owned them, didn't he? True or False?"

"True!"

"What do you mean, true? Just because he owned them didn't keep them from being false, did it?"

"Stanley, you're going around in circles."

"Certainly I go around in circles—but only the best circles!"

"False!"

Self-Made

There once was a guy who went around
       bragging that he was a self-made man.
He gave his wife no credit; he was
       his own exclusive fan.
Finally she had enough of it.
       She told him, "Listen, kiddo,
You'd better knock it off unless
       you want a self-made widow!"
He saw that she meant business.
       So after some feeble laughter,
He shut his big fat mouth and lived
       carefully ever after.

———◆———

HISTORY REWRITTEN MOTHER'S WAY

"Michelangelo! Where do you think you're going?"

"I'm going to paint the ceiling in the Sistine Chapel, Mother."

"What? In your good clothes, you're going to climb up on that rickety scaffold and lie on your back and ruin your eyesight? I won't have it! Besides, you haven't finished painting the back porch, and you promised me a week ago! Now, you're not going *anywhere*, young man, until you've finished your chores!"

———•———

That drum majorette! Let's adopt her!
At twirling batons no one topped her!
   While leading the band
   With baton in each hand
She took off like a small helicopter!

"Did I ever tell you about the time I went out to the Colorado River and shot the rapids?"

"No, Stanley, you didn't. That must have been exciting."

"Not very. They kept right on running—but I only used a .22."

NEW BOOKS

PLAYING DEAD BY LYON STILL

DOWN IN THE DUMPS BY PHELAN M.I.T. LOWE

THAT AIN'T ALL! BY MORRIS CUMMING

LOUDMOUTH
DILLER

Here lies the body of Loudmouth Diller.
Whatever killed him was a real painkiller.

"My grandfather was the kind of man who went to
  a barbershop every day."
"What was he, an actor?"
"No, a barber."

"What's your favorite kind of dog?"
"A hot one."

8

Q. What's a sleeping bag?
A. A nap sack.

One day I was foolish enough to recall the old saying, If a Dog Bites a Man, That's Not News, But If a Man Bites a Dog, That's News!

"Yes, and if you see a man-eating tiger in a zoo, that's not news," said Stanley Winters, "but if you see a man eating tiger in a restaurant, let me know!"

COMIC VALENTINES

A lot of so-called Comic Valentine cards used to be sent out on Saint Valentine's Day. They were a kind of Joke To Tell Your Worst Enemy. For instance:

> You look like an orangutan
>   And you smell like a goat;
> If you were my Valentine
>   I'd cut my throat!

Or this:

Teacher's Pet

> Only someone who's an absolute sap'll
> Give an old crow like our teacher an apple!

Don't ever let your parents tell you kids were nicer in the old days!

OLD JOKES NEVER DIE

He who laughs last doesn't get the joke.

KIDDER
McCANN

> Here lies the body of Kidder McCann;
>   He died laughing.*

---

*At the wrong man.

IT'S GOOD ENOUGH TO EAT

A wonderful tree grows in Denmark. It does not touch the ground but grows above it in space. It's called a Danish space tree.

———•———

Knock! Knock!
Who's there?
Sweets.
Sweets who?
Aw, you guessed!*

———•———

"What became of your balloon?"
"I got a bang out of it!"

"Did you hear about the two flyweights who had a boxing match in a matchbox?" asked Stanley Winters.

"In a matchbox?"

"Yes. They matched the matches, too—they were both redheads. They worked hand in glove. Speaking of boxing gloves, I have a cousin who spends his time boxing gloves. He puts gloves into boxes at the glove factory. Cousin Dozen, we call him, because he puts a dozen pairs in each box."

"Stanley, I'm no match for you today."

"I'm glad you said that—I was about to strike you!"

This had better be read aloud!

11

Home to Stay

Being home is one thing I'm glad about;
Traveling I'm no longer mad about;
   There's nothing bad about it,
   I'm not sad about it,
But I've had about enough as a gadabout!

I OFTEN ORDER IT MYSELF

Once upon a time Old King Cole issued an order to his cooks.

"From now on," he decreed, "chopped cabbage must be mixed with mayonnaise!"

To this day his decree is known as Cole's Law.

The first time I saw Stanley Winters at a party, he had a girl with him who wasn't more than fourteen years old.

"I'd like you to meet my wife," he said, "but she's not here, so how about meeting my daughter?"

A plane that was flying from Rome
To Calcutta was hijacked to Nome.
   The pilot was scared;
   In fact, he declared,
"If you ask me, I shoulda stayed home!"

RARE ITEM

This is the second hand from an old clock, in case anyone is looking for a secondhand second hand.

Said a man by the name of McBudley
Who had moved to a town called West Dudley,
"I'm sorry I came,
'Cause I hate this town's name!"
So he packed up and moved to *East* Dudley!

OLD JOKES NEVER DIE

Deadeye Dick, the world's greatest marksman, loves to entertain his audiences. He aims to please.

Q. What's the worst thing you can find in our school cafeteria?
A. Food.

THE WONDERS OF SCIENCE

Computers can do everything. They can even print books like this one. And since computers never make mistakes, that means that every word in the book will be abS#1u/1Y peR<>Ct.

One day Stanley Winters started talking about fire departments.

"The last town we lived in had the dumbest firemen in the country," he said. "No, that's not true, because we didn't live in the country, we lived in the city—but anyway, they were dumb. One day we had a fire. I rushed over to a neighbor's house and called the fire department.

" 'Help! Help!' I said. 'My house is on fire!'

" 'Where?' asked the fireman.

" 'In the basement!' I told him.

" 'No, I mean how do we get there?'

" 'Don't you still have those big red trucks to ride on?' I asked. What a dummy he was!

" 'Listen!' he said, 'I mean, where are you?'

" 'Across the street at my neighbors!' I told him. What did he think, I was calling from a burning house? I was so disgusted I hung up, and would you believe it, they never came!"

"You mean your house burned down?" I asked, and Stanley sighed.

"You're as bad as they were," he said. "I *told* you the fire started in the basement, so the house burned *up*!"

Q. What does a headhunter have when he kills his first enemy?

A. A head start.

PROBLEM DIFFICULT, MUST SOLVE

Problem: Two sisters. Twins. One named Sue. One known to be a witch. So who's Sue and which's witch?

THE HAPPY MARRIAGE

Every Sunday they bought two newspapers. He did his puzzle, she did hers. That way, not a cross word ever passed between them.

My sister's skin is so tender
she can get a moontan.

Knit-Picker

Nothing I know of
  Would please me better
Than to see a giraffe
  In a turtleneck sweater.

HISTORY REWRITTEN MOTHER'S WAY

"Noah! Why are you building a boat right here on dry land, miles from the water? All the neighbors are laughing at it! They call it Noah's Ark!"

"I've got to finish it and put two of every animal in it, Mother, because we're going to have a flood. It's going to rain for forty days and forty nights."

"Noah, Noah, where do you get these ideas? Forty nights, maybe—a nice frizzly-drizzly shower every night—but forty days? Never! And I don't want you fooling around with all those animals—one of them might bite you! Now, you come in here this minute, and I'll give you some nice chicken soup made from a fresh hen and a rooster."

"Mom! Those were the chickens for my boat!"

The family next door to the Tabors
Often threatens the Tabors with sabres,
        And shouts, "Get thee hence!"
        Across the back fence.
They are not what I'd call good neighbors.

Stanley Winters was standing at the salad bar, staring at the Thousand Island dressing and muttering to himself.

"Something the matter, Stanley?"

"Shh! I'm counting!"

THE LEGEND OF SNICKENHAMMERSTEIN

One dark and stormy night, a traveler lost his way in the forest of Snickenhammerstein. Finally, through the driving rain, he saw a large, crumbling house. He rang the bell. Slow footsteps dragged toward the door. A grotesque, malformed old man opened it. He agreed to let the traveler stay for the night, and showed him upstairs to a large, shadowy room with an enormous bed in it.

"I be all alone here now. And this be the very room the master went mad in and died these many years ago," said the grotesque, malformed old man. "Since then, every year on the anniversary of his death, someone has died in this room!"

"Oh?" said the traveler. "And when is the next anniversary?"

The old man gave him a sly, frightened look and said, "This very night!"

The grotesque, malformed old man had no more than spoken before he suddenly reeled back, clutched at his throat, let out a terrible groan, and toppled over.

The traveler sprang to his side and felt his pulse.

"By George!" he exclaimed. "Well, that takes care of *that*!"

He covered the body reverently with a bed-spread, moved his things to another room, and got a good night's sleep.

Moral: We never know who's next.

NEW BOOK

———•———

You Would Have Liked Them

Bishop Thomas Xavier Foley
   Tended to be holy;
Bishop Martin Ignatius Grolier
   Tended to be holier;
But neither one, I'll vow,
   Was holier-than-thou.

———•———

Stanley Winters and I were listening to a newscast.

"Today," said the newscaster, "is the birthday of the inventor of the telephone—"

"Alexander Graham Buzzer," said Stanley.

"Bell!" I said. "Bell!"

"My telephone never rings," said Stanley. "When I get a call my secretary buzzes me, so naturally I think of him as—"

"All right, all right!"

My Aunt Clementine was so tough
she was the den mother in an opium den!

———•———

An amorous E.T. named Petey
Signed an intergalactic treaty
    Which gave him the right
    To unlimited flight
With his extraterrestrial sweetie!

———•———

DESMOND M.
McWHIRTY

Here lies the body of Desmond McWhirty,
Whose dastardly deeds were dark and dirty;
His middle name was Macmillan,
But in spite of that, he was a villain.

———•———

WALTER
WEST

Here lies the body of Walter West;
As a pickpocket Walt was considered the best.
He was doing fine till he tried something new—
He tried his tricks on a kangaroo.

———•———

    Professor Moriarty
       Never gave a party.
    He thought them a waste of time
       And preferred a life of crime.

———•———

The Egotist's Lament

It's tough to be so handsome;
   You wouldn't think I'd care,
But the jealous looks of you average schnooks
   Are hard for me to bear.
It's rough to be so clever;
   I *wish* I weren't so resourceful,
For the jealous fits of you lesser wits
   Can make me feel remorseful.
It's awful to be so popular;
   I suppose the attention should gladden me,
But the jealous sighs of you average guys
   Have been known on occasion to sadden me.
It's a burden to be so outstanding,
   But I guess it was just meant to be.
Though I wish I could change things,
     I can't rearrange things;
   It's just that I'm—well—gorgeous ME!

Q. What's an honest king?
A. A straight ruler.

NEW CRIME NOVELS

I'll Rub You Out!   *I Confess*
by Annie Racer   by I. Dunham Inne

Doorway to Death
by Hugo Furst

Stanley Winters was showing me his family album. He pointed to a stern-looking old gent with a lot of whiskers.

"This one is my great-grandfather. What's so great about *him*?"

"That's just an expression, Stanley."

"You mean that look on his face?"

"No, no, I'm talking about the 'great' part."

"You mean the one in his hair?"

"Now, listen, Stanley! For instance, I might say I had a great-aunt—"

"Go ahead, say it. Maybe it's even true. But what made her great? Did she invent something? I never had a great-aunt, but I had a small aunt; I'll bet she wasn't more than 4 feet 2 in her stocking feet and 4 feet 1 barefoot—she wore thick stockings—"

I didn't stay to hear any more.

BAD JOKES WE MUST NEVER TELL AGAIN

1. In winter, a bald Indian wears a fur hat to keep his wigwam.
2. The thousands of fat people who eat Fig Newtons gain new tons every day.
3. If you see a cannibal coming, keep cool. That's the important thing—don't get in a stew.
4. Any joke in this book.

How Can You Hiss With a Lisp?

When a serpent who's lisped all his life
Tries to introduce friends to his wife,
   The poor serpent hiththeth,
   "Thith ith the miththuth!"
Which causes much marital strife.

Q. In cannibal language, what's the word for *midgets*?

A. *Snacks*.

Stanley Winters asked me why I was hobbling around.

"Bad back," I snapped. "Haven't you ever had any back trouble?"

"No, but a friend of mine has," said Stanley. "He's a football coach. His new fullback is in terrible shape, but that's nothing. Once his team spent a million dollars on a new player and only got a quarter back—a real two-bit player."

HISTORY REWRITTEN MOTHER'S WAY

"William, where are you going?"

"I'm going to cross the channel and conquer England, Mother, so that everyone will call me William the Conqueror."

"What? Now you listen to me, William. You *know* how rough that English Channel gets, and you *know* you get seasick even in a rowboat! I won't have it, do you hear?"

"Aw, Mom!"

They Have Poor Posture, Too

Amoebas tend to be slobs.
Nothing much but blobs.
Let's face it, your average amoeba
Ain't no Queen of Sheba.

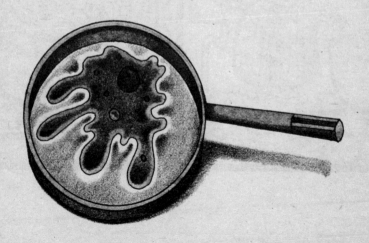

Yours May, But Ours Won't

When rabbits become known
    For their great lack of breeding,
And turtles get tickets
    For dangerous speeding,
And elephants all
    Are forced to tie strings
In a bow round their trunks
    To remind them of things,
When wise old owls start
    Making stupid remarks,
And watchdogs' bites start
    To be worse than their barks,
When pigs start to diet
    And go on half-rations,
And cows don't come home
    But go on vacations,
Then maybe a great thing will
    Happen in turn: It's—your
Cat will stop sharpening
    Claws on the furniture!

"Yesterday I saw an old lady help a Boy Scout across the street," said Stanley Winters. "He had a sprained ankle. And on the other side of the street, a man was holding up a bank."

"What?" I cried.

"That's right. He was selling piggy banks, and he was holding one up and saying, 'Save your money!' So I didn't buy one—I saved my money. Then he said, 'Buy Now and Save Later!' So then I bought one. He was also selling safety razors. He showed one to the Boy Scout and said, 'Buy Now and Shave Later!' "

"What did the Boy Scout do?"

"He said, 'No, sell it to my kid brother—he's a little shaver right now!' "

Q. What does someone have who twitches?
A. A nervous tic.
Q. And what does a dog have when his master gets the tweezers?
A. A nervous tick.

———•———

THAT CHEESE-AND-TOMATO LOOK

Once there was a terrible man named Peter Putrid, who had the Evil Eye. He could take one look at you and zap you. Everyone was afraid of Pete's Zap Eye.

———•———

THE ROBIN'S MISTAKE

One night a robin was sitting around in his nest, watching TV.

A TV star on a talk show said, "An old proverb we all should remember is this: The Early Bird Catches the Worm."

The robin was so impressed that instead of getting up at his usual time, around dawn, he set his alarm clock for 3 A.M.

At 3 A.M. he flew down to the ground to look for a worm, but it was so dark he couldn't see a thing, and he was tired all the rest of the day.

Moral: Don't believe everything you hear on TV.

Fifty-Fifty

One thing I'm sure would make me stare:
  If I should see somewhere someday
A centipede sitting down in a chair
  And crossing his legs in a casual way.

———•———

My Uncle Herbert is such a time-waster
he tells hair-raising stories to bald men.

———•———

OLD JOKES NEVER DIE
Knock!
Who's there?
Opportunity.

I should never have shown Stanley Winters the watch I got for my birthday.

"Very nice," said Stanley. "There's no present like the time. Years ago my grandfather gave me his clock—I call it a grandson's clock now—but the only trouble is, it runs backward. Instead of going *tick-tock,* it goes *tock-tick*. And have you ever seen a banjo clock? It's shaped just like a banjo, and instead of going *tick-tock* it goes *plinkety-plink*. I even had a stammering banjo clock once that went *p-plinkety p-plink*. Otherwise it was a perfectly normal banjo clock. It had an hour hand—that was the first hand, and a minute hand—that was the second hand, and a second hand—but that made the second hand the third hand! I've never understood that. Somehow it puts me in mind of a man in a circus sideshow who ate razor blades and broken glass. Once he ate a clock, but he didn't like it. It was time-consuming. Which reminds me—did you hear about the railway station clock that struck eleven? It fell off the roof and hit a football team!"

Two cannibals sat down at a table in a cannibal restaurant. The waiter said, "Do you mind sharing your dinner? All we have left is a missionary from Prague. You can each pay for half."

"Okay," said the cannibals, "we'll split the Czech."

———•———

It Happened in Brazil

A grass snake from Rio, Maximilian,
Was adored by a girl snake named Lilian,
    But the snake-in-the-grass
    Snuck away from the lass!
What a rotten reptilian Brazilian!

———•———

I'm a Fair-Minded Fellow

I lost a dime today.
    It isn't fair!
Had a rotten time today.
    It isn't fair!
The floor was waxed. I slipped,
I stumbled, tripped and flipped.
My brand-new slacks got ripped.
    It isn't fair!

There's a special show, I'm told.
    It isn't fair!
'Cause the tickets are all sold.
    It isn't fair!
What's that? My Cousin Fred
Is home and sick in bed
And I get to go instead?
    Now, *that* is fair!

Stanley Winters caught me reading the sports page.

"Here's a story about a ballplayer who used to be a burglar," I told him.

"I read it," said Stanley. "He's the only ballplayer who ever stole first. Too bad he wasn't a ballplayer first, then he could have stolen second."

"Now, listen, Stanley—!"

"Yes, yes, it's getting late, so I'd better steal home."

My sister is so dumb
she thinks a high school has to be on a hill.

The Fidgety Type

I used to think planes were all right,
But I *hated* my bargain-fare flight
    To Butte and Tacoma
    And Sludge, Oklahoma—
I only stayed *there* overnight!

"One time I worked for a company that built elevators," said Stanley Winters. "The last one we built had fifty buttons."

"You mean it was built for a fifty-story building?"

"That's right. But as luck would have it, someone in the order department got mixed up, and it was installed in a ten-story bank building. The day it was ready, the president of the bank got in and said, 'Hey, we only have ten floors, but this elevator has buttons for fifty floors! What happens if I push the "50" button?' As the doors closed, he was pushing the '50' button."

"What happened?"

Stanley sighed.

"Blast-off! Right through the roof!"

A fish that was caught up in Michigan
Said, "If I could have only one wish again,
    I'd want a vacation,
    Then reincarnation,
And come back as some kind of fish again!"

———•———

Q. What animal lives in the center of Antarctica?
A. A polecat with a Southern accent.

———•———

Who Is It?

The Thing that appears is mysterious;
I sometimes believe I'm delirious;
 I don't know how near It is
 When suddenly—here It is!
The situation's quite serious.

"Did you know I used to act in amateur the-atricals?" asked Stanley Winters. "One time I was supposed to produce a box of matches from my pocket and light the leading lady's ciga-rette. Well, I couldn't produce. I'd forgotten to bring them!"

"What did you do, Stanley?"

Naturally he said, "I gave a matchless per-formance!"

NOBODY'S NICE ANYMORE

In the old days the joke went like this:

A man comes out of a hotel and says to the door-man, "Call me a cab!"

"Yes, sir," says the doorman. "You're a cab!"

Today it's different:

A man comes out of a hotel and says to the door-man, "Call me a cab!"

The doorman, who is busy talking to a friend, gives him a dirty look and says, "I'll call you worse than that if you don't stop bugging me!"

VINCENT
McVICKERS

Here lies the body of Vincent McVickers;
He had one of those irritating snickers.

HISTORY REWRITTEN MOTHER'S WAY

"Charles! What are you doing in that little airplane?"

"I'm going to fly across the Atlantic Ocean to Paris, Mother, and become the first man to fly across the ocean alone."

"What? Charles Lindbergh, are you out of your mind? Paris! All those French girls—why, I'd worry myself sick! Now, you wait right here, I'm going with you! I'll not have you roaming around Paris, France, all alone with no mother to look out for you! I'll pack a nice picnic lunch, and—"

Glad To Oblige

Is it true you're disgusted?
   Do these jokes really pain you?
Feel free to leave.
   Don't let me detain you.
You detest such low humor?
   You find it a strain?
You'd like to be lifted
   To a much higher plane?
Sit down. I'll come through
   With my usual aplomb:
Under your chair
   Is planted—a bomb!

HOW TO
GET RICH
BY
MARIAN
MONEY
Life Is a
Bore
by
Dulles
Dishwater
HARD TO
DECIDE
BY
MAYER
MAYNOTT

NEW BOOKS

A gnome and a gnat met a gnu;
Said the gnat, "Sir, it's gnice to gnow *you*!"
    Said the gnome, "Sir, to me,
    Our unusual G
Is gneat!" The gnu gnodded. "Me, too!"

Balloonists have to stay good friends. They can't afford to have a falling-out.

We were walking a nature trail with a forest ranger who pointed to a group of trees and said, "Now, there's a mighty fine stand of fir trees."

I left at that point, because Stanley Winters was saying something about wanting fir-stand information.

OLD JOKES NEVER DIE

"I went home for the weekend."
"Did you? And how did you find your family?"
"Oh, I just drove up to the house
   and there they were."

———•———

MODERN TIMES FOR GREAT LOVERS

"Marry me, Juliet," said Romeo, "and I'll support you in style! I'll bring home the bacon!"

"Bacon?" cried Juliet. "Why, don't you know bacon is terrible for us? It's full of nitrites, and—"

"Well, anyway," said Romeo, "I'll be our bread-winner. I'll earn our bread and butter!"

"Romeo, you're impossible!" sighed Juliet. "Bread and butter are both fattening, and butter is loaded with cholesterol. You've got to bring home something that's full of healthy nutriments!"

So poor Romeo went out and worked for peanuts.

———•———

Q. What do you call it when a dentist works on teeth
. on a yacht?
A. Off-shore drilling.

---•---

Tale of a Crook

He *claimed* that his name was Sharkey.
He was caught with another man's car key.
    Said he, "I would *never*
    Have took his car, *ever!*"
Which, of course, was a lot of malarkey.*

---•---

*And also some pretty bad grammar.
I'm glad that he went to the slammer.†
†Slammer *means* jail;
End of the tale.

Napoleon Bonaparte
  Once took a phone apart.
Al Bell resented it,
  Since he hadn't yet invented it.

It was once said in Constantinople,
"Our sultan's the dumb kind you hope'll
    Split the seat of his pants—
    And there's always a chance,
'Cause if anyone'll do it, that dope'll!"

NEW BOOK

Putting on the Brakes
by Sloan Down

Q. What does an art class model have?
A. A drawn look.

The other day I thought Stanley Winters said, "One thing about pizza, it's much easier to sell when it's much easier."

"Stanley, you're not making sense!"

"*You're* not listening! I said it's much easier to sell when it's much cheesier!"

VITAL STATISTICS

Did you know that 8 out of every 10 people are part of 80% of the population?

HISTORY REWRITTEN MOTHER'S WAY

"George! What are you doing in that boat?"

"I'm going to cross the Delaware, Mother, and defeat the Hessian troops in Trenton."

"What? Do you realize that river is full of ice? George Washington, you come right back here— you'll catch your death of cold!"

Greedy Birthday Kid

Never mind what you gave me last;
    That's ancient history.
On my birthday I always forget the past;
    It's the present that counts with me!

Hard Luck Story

I saw a four-leaf clover,
    But my luck was out of whack;
For when I bent over to pick the clover,
    I got a crick in my back!

"One time when I was playing in a jazz band, we finally got our big chance," said Stanley Winters. "We were hired to play at a penthouse party. When we walked into the building, we were determined to make good."

"And did you?"

"Certainly! We got in the elevator and rose to the occasion."

Though my aunt was a terrible cook,
As a tyrant she had what it took;
    When she baked awful gook,
    She would give us a look,
And we'd still have to gobbledegook!

LITTLE-KNOWN AMERICAN HISTORY

During the War of 1812, American cannons on shore sank a British frigate with a single volley. The Americans celebrated with a big dance they called the Volley Ball.

NEW BOOKS

Guess Whodunit?
by Ike Onfess

Thirty-Six Hours
by Dana Haff

Button Your Lip!
by Candy Chatter

Broomstick Shift

A witch who lives in our town
Is famous near and far;
Once she was nearly arrested
For driving without a car!

"My pet died, and I can't understand it! He was the picture of health!"
"You must have been looking at the negative."

It was foolish of me to ask Stanley Winters what he thought of the metric system.

"For me, it doesn't measure up," he said. "All those decimal pints—"

"You mean decimal *points,* don't you, Stanley?"

"If I did, I'd say so. A decimal pint is half a liter."

"What about meters? Do you like them as well as yards?"

"Not to play in. Your average meter doesn't even have a tree in it, let alone a swing. By the way, do you know how to measure Up? First you get a long tape measure. You hold one end on the ground, and attach a balloon to the other end—"

By then I was halfway to the door.

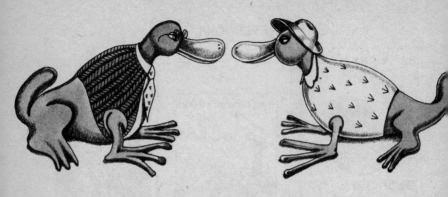

He Always Called His Wife Puss;
It Was a Sort of Nickname, See?

To his wife said a duckbill platypus,
"I'll admit your friend Ethel's a fatty, Puss,
But don't call her chubby
In front of her hubby—
I hate when you women get catty, Puss!"

———•———

MODERN TIMES IN THE GARDEN OF EDEN

Serpent: Here, Eve, try this apple. It's delicious!
Eve: Heavens, no. My doctor says I'm allergic to apples! I'll just have one of those kumquats, thank you.

———•———

OLD JOKES NEVER DIE

People who live in glass houses
shouldn't throw parties.

———•———

BASEBALL SEASON

On opening day, a bigwig threw out the first ball. Then the shortstop threw out the first batter. There was a big argument about the play, and the umpire threw out the first manager. And that was the way it went threw-out the season.

NEW BOOKS

By Gosh! By Golly!
by George Bygum

I'll Get There Somehow!
by Hooker Crook

How I Became a Saint
by Doone Goode

It's a Dog's Life
by Ima K. Nine

The Most and the Least
by Maxie & Minnie Mum

THOSE WERE SOME BIRTHDAY PARTIES!

When I was a kid, we were so tough
we played Pin the Tail on the Donkey
with a real donkey!

One time when I was sick in bed and couldn't get away, Stanley Winters came to see me.

"I need a doctor," I grumbled, "but mine doesn't make house calls."

"Mine won't make house calls, either," said Stanley, "but he makes marvelous bird calls—even the birds are fooled. Of course, it comes naturally—he's a quack. Know something? Once I tried to question a duck, but he ducked the question!"

Nature abhors a vacuum, and so does our cleaning lady. And by the way—if there's nothing in a vacuum to begin with, how can you get a vacuum cleaner?

———•———

Diet? Try It!

There are two possibilities,
　　And do you like either?
Let food go to waste
　　Or to waist? Me, neither!

———•———

Of *course* I bite my fingernails! What do you ex-
pect me to do—bite someone else's?

———•———

Dumb Bunny

Have you ever used a dictionary,
　　My little honeybun?
I can tell by your diction—
　　Nary a one!

———•———

Absentminded? Me?

I had a whatchamacallit,
　　The loveliest whatzit I've seen.
It's one of those something-or-others—
　　Surely you know what I mean!
When I think of that thingamajig,
　　I'm absolutely appalled,
Since now I can't even remember
　　Where I put it, whatever it's called!

———•———

HISTORY REWRITTEN MOTHER'S WAY

"Hannibal, what are you doing out here looking at the elephants?"

"I'm going to march them and my soldiers up through the Alps and down into Italy, Mother, and beat the daylights out of the Romans."

"What? Hannibal Hamilcar, are you out of your mind? When I think what just one elephant costs, and you're talking about— Honestly, I just don't know what gets into you kids these days! Now, you can't have the keys to the elephant cage, and that's final!"

———•———

How To Get To My Place

Turn off the Turnpike
    At Exit 4-E;
Turn right at the stoplight
    Then left on Route 3;
Watch for the white church,
    Bear left on Burt Road,
And just past the town hall
    You'll see a dirt road;
Turn *right* on the dirt road
    And watch for a big farm
(You'll know when you smell it,
    It's Peterson's Pig Farm);
Go on to the graveyard,
    And past the town pump,
And next on your right
    Will come the town dump;
Now, my house will be
    The next one you see there;
But don't look for me,
    Because I won't *be* there.

CHRISTOPHER
NYE

Here lies the body of Christopher Nye,
Whose family motto was Never Say Die!
        So he never said it.
        He did it.

The Vegetable Hater

Only a meanie
  Could relish zucchini.
I turn pale
  Around kale.
A carrot?
  Can't bear it.
Between me and spinach
  It's a fight to the finach.
Lettuce
  Is out to get us.
No beet
  Is fit to eat.
Artichokes
  Are Nature's bad jokes.
The Brussels sprout
  Deserves a drought.
Cauliflower
  Makes me glower.
Parsley
  Is gharsley!
Parsnips must go!
  Peas? Oh, no!
Any veggie
  Makes me edgy!

HISTORY REWRITTEN MOTHER'S WAY

"Christopher! Where are you going in that sailor suit?"

"I'm going to sail westward, Mother, and discover the New World."

"What? Christopher Columbus, have you got water on the brain now? When are you going to stop listening to those dingdongs who say the world is round? It's flat, flat, flat; anybody with two eyes in his head can see that. And if you go sailing west, you're going to sail right off the edge! My baby! I'd never see you again! Besides, we've got enough trouble with *this* world; who needs a new one? Now, sit down at the table. Momma's going to bake you a nice lasagna just the way you like it—and forget all those crazy ideas!"

OLD JOKES NEVER DIE

Indian restaurants curry favor
with those who favor curry.

"I made a bad mistake yesterday," said Stanley Winters. "I bought a box of sordid chocolates."

"Stanley, you mean *assorted*—"

"No, these were all the same, and disgusting!"

MAXWELL
MAX

Here lies the body of Maxwell Max;
Somebody parted his hair with an ax.

————•————

NEW BOOKS

You Really Enjoyed That!
by Major Day

Is Your Family Well?
by Howard DeFolks

————•————

YES, BUT . . .

Roses are red,
   except when they're pink or yellow or white.
Violets are blue,
   except for some African violets.
Sugar is sweet,
   though some sugars are sweeter than others.
   Now you take fructose: Fructose is 18%
   sweeter than lactose, or maybe it's the other
   way around.
And so are you,
   which means you'd better cut down on
   those candy bars!

---●---

How To Have
A Long and Happy Life

I'll never best
  Mount Everest;
You won't catch *me*
  At the bottom of the sea;
My car's never thundered
  In the Indy 500;
The Antarctic waste
  Is not to my taste;
Just the sight of a trapeze
  Gives me watery knees;
To antagonize guys twice my size
  Is unwise;
To you I'm entrusting
  Bronco-busting;
My rating as a hero
  Is a comfortable zero.
Which is why, if you've wondered,
  I'll live to be a hundred.

---●---

Q. What's a quarrel between sci-fi writers?
A. Science friction.

"Can you imagine?" cried Stanley Winters.
"The phone company had the nerve to send me
a bill!"
  "Did you pay it?"
  "Certainly not! I believe in free speech!"

OLD JOKES NEVER DIE

Q. What is America's favorite food beginning with A?

A. A hamburger.

That's the worst joke I've ever heard!

Funny, Ain't It?

Watching somebody else slip on the ice
  Is funny, but can't hold a candle
To seeing some other guy step on a rake
  And get hit on the nose by the handle;
When somebody else falls flat on his face,
  I'm the first one to slap his knee;
So when somebody slips or stumbles or falls,
  Why don't I laugh if it's *me?*

> "Yesterday I had a terrible day mare," said Stanley Winters.
>
> "You mean a nightmare, don't you, Stanley?"
>
> "No, I went to a riding academy where they rent horses by the day, and—"

How I Disgraced Myself
in the Auditorium

School play.
Had to stay.
Bored.
Snored.

———•———

A long time ago there were a lot of use-a-word-in-a-sentence jokes, as for instance:

Use the word *discos* in a sentence.
It discos to show how bad things can get.

Or the word *curlicue*.
You can't shoot good pool with a curlicue.

As you can see, these were almost as bad as knock-knock jokes. However, to use the word *knockwurst* in a sentence:

An elephant joke is bad, a sentence joke is worse, but I'd rate a knock-knockwurst.

———•———

CHINESE FOOD

Everyone in the world likes Chinese food.

You don't believe it? I'll prove it to you!

First of all, 1/4 of the human race is Chinese. That's 25% right there who like Chinese food.

Next: Among the 3 out of 4 people who are not Chinese, at least half like Chinese food. If they didn't, there wouldn't be so many Chinese restaurants. So that's half of 3/4, which is 3/8, which is another 37.5%.

Now, Chinese people only like Chinese food, and half of all the other people think they don't like Chinese food. They like Italian food, especially spaghetti, which is why there are so many Italian restaurants.

But spaghetti was invented in China. Marco Polo brought it back to Italy from China. So if half the people who aren't Chinese like spaghetti, that's another 37.5%, and what have we got?

Chinese who like Chinese food: 25 % of the
human
race.

Other people who like it: 37.5%
People who like spaghetti: + 37.5%
                           ───────────
                             100 %

What did I tell you?

Up a Tree!

It's been a lifelong embarrassment:
   For some fool reason or other,
All my life I've never been able
   To tell one tree from another.
That elms and oaks are different
   I can see without a hitch;
I only have one problem—
   I can't tell which is which.
If you stood me on a scaffold
   And put my neck in a noose,
I couldn't tell willow from chestnut,
   I couldn't tell pine from spruce.
Many's the painful hour I've spent
   In botanical gardens and parks
Doing my best to memorize leaves
   And remember the pattern of barks.
Yet whenever I come across a tree
   It's the same old feeling of shame
As I say, "Your bark is familiar,
   But I can't remember your name!"

"Last night at dinner," said Stanley Winters, "somebody asked me who was the twenty-second president of the United States. Do you know who it was?"

"Who?"

"Cousin Agnes! She asked me, but I didn't know."

HISTORY REWRITTEN MOTHER'S WAY

"Paul! What are you doing up at this hour?"

"I'm going to take a horseback ride, Mother, to warn the patriots that the British are coming!"

"What? At midnight? Paul Revere, you get right back in that bed!"

———•———

My uncle Jud is so mean
he goes to parades
just to stand in front of short people.

———•———

LEONARD
TERSE

Here lies the body of Leonard Terse;
Driving too fast, took a turn for the worse.

———•———

STAN AND FRAN
A Primer Story

Fran said, "Stan, see the man."

Stan said, "Fran, the man has a pan. See the pan the man has."

The man said, "What pan are you little twits talking about? If you're talking about my face, I'll knock your heads together!"

Stan and Fran ran.

Watch That Glass!

Children who are able
  To sit at the table
With glasses of milk when there's company
  Shouldn't dump any.

NEW BOOKS

I'll Bet He Can!   *Winning Is Everything*
by Betty Kant   by Fowler Fairmeans

Q. What can you do when your house is too small and you need twice as much room?

A. Get a typewriter and double-space.

"I hate it when autumn leaves are falling," said Stanley Winters. "Because when autumn leaves leave the trees is when autumn leaves, and then we get winter."

"And what's worse than winter? Winters!"

For once I had the last word.